KUMIHIMO Mastery

Unleash Your Creativity with Step by Step Pictures for Effortless Braided and Beaded Patterns Book

Sylvie C Erastus

Table of Contents

CHAPTER ONE

GETTING STARTED WITH KUMIHIMO

What is Kumihimo?

Kumi himo is a Japanese term that translates as "gathered threads". It is the art of braiding cords, threads, ribbons, strands of beads, and jewelry wire into beautiful ropes. These ropes, also known as kumihimo, are strong yet slim and versatile.

History of Kumihimo

Kumihimo is an old skill dating all the way back to the sixth century. The old art forms stretch all the way back to well over 1300 years. Due to the perishable nature of braid materials and the secrecy surrounding braiding techniques, the early history of Kumihimo is difficult to study. Not until around 400 years ago were braid designs published.

Kumihimo braids have been utilized in a variety of ways throughout Japanese history. Buddhism introduced braiding to Japan, where it was used in clothing and rituals. Kumihimo braids were later heavily used into Samurai armor and weapons, as well as kimono attire.

The obi, the traditional belt of the kimono, was traditionally wrapped with a kumihimo string called an obijime. It is a work of art that is both culturally relevant and aesthetically pleasing.

In recent history, the art has had a regeneration because to Makiko Tada's development of the foam Kumihimo disk and plate.

Initially, the operation was carried out totally by hand, without the use of any instrument. Generally, the early kumihimo are monochromatic or have a very restricted color palette.

Later on, weavers developed tools that let them to create more complex patterns, allowing producers to use additional colors. The original kumihimo looms, known as takadai and marudai, are somewhat huge and heavy, as well as quite immovable.

What is kumihimo Used for?

Kumihimo was originally used to embellish Buddhist scrolls and other religious items. They were subsequently used to connect Samurai armour and Kimonos.

While they are still used to decorate sacred artifacts and kimonos, they are also available as necklaces, bracelets, and even wall art. Kumihimo works became famous as tourist gifts due to their trendy and sophisticated presentation of a traditional Japanese art method.

Additionally, in recent years, an increasing number of individuals have gravitated into Kumihimo in search of opportunities to produce their own works. From friendship bracelets to necklaces, from bags to wall art, the sight and feel of Kumihimo creations captivates the public.

Different shapes and patterns may be created by modifying the braiding material, the thickness or number of strands, the shape of the disk against the square plate, and by adding beads to your kumihimo braid.

Kumihimo can withstand a great deal of wear and tear due to the fact that it is made up of several strands of robust and resilient silk. It produces a strange yet durable dog leash, handbag strap, or belt. The process of weaving kumihimo from several strands allows for an infinite number of color combinations.

CHAPTER TWO

TOOLS USED FOR KUMIHIMO

As is the case with other favorite beading methods, kumihimo may be done with an almost infinite number of materials. Before you begin your first beaded kumihimo project, ensure that you have a few essential items on available to ensure a satisfactory outcome. We'll go over all of the kumihimo braiding materials you'll need to get started with this great hobby in this section.

Kumihimo Disks

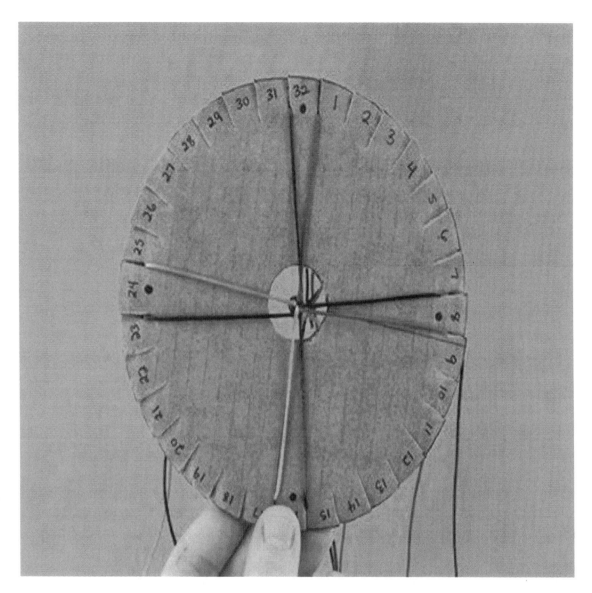

In the beading world, a disk is utilized for Kumihimo. For novices, foam kumihimo disks are ideal. They're inexpensive, you can write on them to indicate your location, and they're lightweight and extremely portable. Disks come in a variety of forms and sizes, depending on the kind of project you're working on.

kumihimo disks are available in two shapes: round and square. Circular foam kumihimo disks in 6″ and 4″ sizes are often used to create round braids with a hollow central core. To create a flat braid suited for a flat bracelet, a square kumihimo disk is utilized.

Additionally, you may purchase disks in a variety of sizes. This has no effect on the completed braid. However, you may discover that you are more at ease with bigger disks — or with smaller disks. This is very dependent on the size of your hands and how you hold your work. As a result, the size is irrelevant when you first begin. However, as you gain skill, you may like to experiment with other sizes.

You'll notice that the disks are numbered and include a hole in the center. What you probably cannot see as well are the grooved edges.

Square Kumihimo Disc
www.myworldofbeads.com

As a result, when you configure the disk, you will be prompted to thread your wire through precise numbered grooves. Because the cords cross in the center, the braided cord will flow downward through the central hole as you braid.

Kumihimo Bobbins

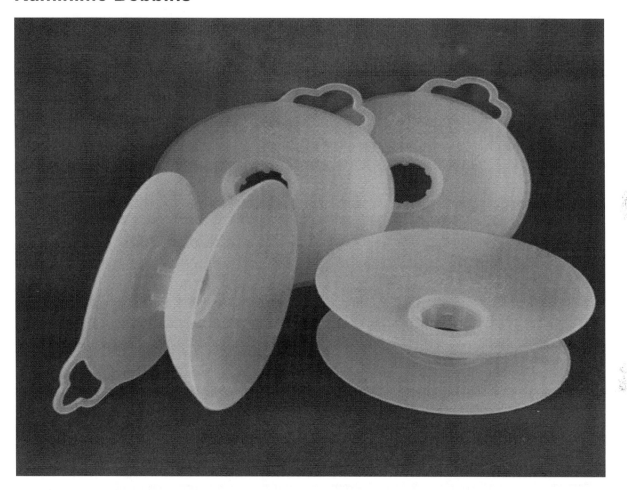

Bobbins were the other essential Kumihimo item that is needed. Braiding consumes a significant amount of cable. Thus, even if you're making a bracelet for a little wrist, you'll need an extremely lengthy piece of string.

While you work, all of your wires will be dangling from the disk's outside border. As a result, if you leave them hanging free, they will quickly get tangled as you move the cords about to construct the braid.

That is where bobbins come into play . A set of plastic bobbins is required to handle the many strands and to secure any beads in place when braiding. Each cable may be wound onto a bobbin. Thus, instead of large lengths of thread, you now have bobbins dangling from the borders of your disk. Simply unwind the line as needed, and tangled cords are a thing of the past!.

The good thing about all of this is that the bobbins and even the weight may be used in a variety of different craft projects. There are different sizes of bobbins available. Thus, even if your rope has beads, you can still wound everything into a bobbin to avoid tangles!

Again, as a general guideline, ensure that your collection of beading materials includes one pair of bobbins for each foam loom.Try to maintain one pair of bobbins for each foam kumihimo disc in your beading equipment collection so that you may work on many projects concurrently.

Weights

As you work, your braid will drop through the disk's core hole so having a weight to lead it through is quite beneficial. Additionally, this assists you in achieving a more balanced tension. You may use a homemade objec as a beginner. However, it is advisable to get a weight as you get used to the craft to make your work fast and easy.

Kumihimo Weight
www.myworldofbeads.com

Attach the weight to your combined cables at their point of intersection, in the center of the disk's hole. As you work, the weight hangs below and will continue to draw your finished braid down.

Kumihimo Cord

There are several cable alternatives to choose from when creating a kumihimo braid, both with and without beads.

If you're building a kumihimo braid using large-hole beads I'd recommend using a little thinner cable to ensure that all eight strands pass through the center hole of the focal bead.

To highlight a focal bead or a unique pair of end caps, you may use satin rat tail cord in thicknesses ranging from 0.5mm to 3mm. The vibrant hues of these silky cords will result in an incredibly beautiful final kumihimo braid. However, keep in mind that a thicker satin string will cause the slots in your foam kumihimo discs to enlarge.

Another excellent material for kumihimo braids is leather cord. Leather may be utilized to create both men's and women's kumihimo jewelry, as well as more rustic and Bohemian-style pieces.

Kumihimo end caps and claps

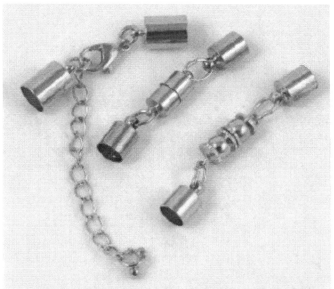

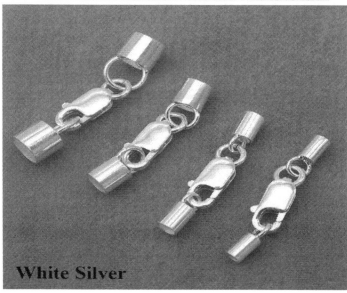

White Silver

Decorative end caps may be used to cover the ends of your kumihimo braids, depending on your personal preference. End caps are available in a wide range of forms, metals, and colors, ranging from very big to extremely tiny.

Kumihimo Beads

Some may say that the beads are the most appealing aspect of beaded kumihimo—and I would agree! And here is when the real fun begins: selecting your kumihimo bead material. Your completed creation will be uniquely yours due to the beads!

A few tubes of size 6 seed beads is sufficient for starting beaded kumihimo projects. Once you've mastered the art of beading your kumihimo braids, explore with 3mm fire-polished glass beads, 3mm round glass druks, lightweight gemstone beads, pearls, or even antique German and Czech glass beads. For maximum glitz, invest in crystal beads or stock up on affordable Chinese crystals to create gorgeous beaded kumihimo ropes right out of the 1920s.

Kumihimo Loom

The Kumi Loom disc itself makes kumihimo weaving a very relaxing pastime. The notches around the loom's outside edge are numbered, and the weaver inserts a silken strand into them. Another strand is taken in by a notch on the other side, and so on until all strands are in place. The weaving then starts.

Weaving kumihimo is as easy as counting using the KumiLoom. To begin, the weaver inserts a silk strand into the slot below and to the right. Following that, the direction is upward and to the left. Finally, the whole loom receives a left turn. It's astonishing that this simple three-step method can result in such intricate designs as kumihimo.

Guidelines for kumihimo Weaving

The following are the most fundamental guidelines you should be aware of.

• To straighten curly nylon cables, gently steam them. This will significantly simplify the process of stringing your beads.

• String beads onto the cords using a large-eye needle. Alternatively, you may dip the cord ends in Super Glue gel and let to dry to thread beads without the need of a needle.

• Slit a 12" slit on the rear of each bobbin to secure the cord ends.

Using a kumihimo stand enables you to braid with both hands, rather as holding your disk in one hand and stringing beads and braiding with the other. Your tension will be more consistent, and the overall appearance of your product will be more professional. Additionally, if you are interrupted, a kumihimo stand provides a tangle-free method to store your creation.

• If you are stopped during the braiding process, just shift the bottom-left cord to the top position and leave it there. You'll have three cords at the top position, and you'll always know precisely where to restart your project. When you restart, pull the top right cable down, quarter-turn the disk, and continue.

• Note on gauge: Not all beads are made equal! While the gauge for size 8° seed beads is typically 6 per braided inch, this formula will not always work. The only way to determine if a certain color or finish will work with this recipe is to do a test braid. Take note of any required adjustments to gauge and make any adjustments to your design.

CHAPTER THREE

HOW TO BEGIN WITH KUMIHIMO

Basic Round Braid with 8 Warps

This method involves the use of a variety of looms to create a variety of braids. This lesson demonstrates a simple circular braid with eight warps.

When practicing Kumihimo, you will discover that varying the quantity of strands and the color of the strands alters the overall appearance. Changing the stringing material and adding beads to all or portion of the strands may also alter the appearance. Bear in mind that you may not want to use a stretchy stringing material.

Each thread in a single "slit" is referred to as a warp in Kumihimo. We'll be using a round Kumihimo disk with 32 slots to make an eight-warp basic round braid in this tutorial. When gauging stringing material, a decent rule of thumb is to multiply the desired length by three. This will work for the majority of designs, unless you are using bigger beads, in which case the length may need to be adjusted. After you've mastered the basic circle braid, learn how to embellish Kumihimo with beads.

INSTRUCTIONS

Step One -Setting up the Disk

Gather all eight strands and secure one end with a knot. If you're working with extra-long lengths, we recommend utilizing bobbins to prevent tangling.

Step two

Insert the knotted end into the Kumihimo disk's center hole.

Step three

Divide the strands into four groups of two and put them over the disk at the black location marks. When configuring the disk, place the number 32 at the top.

Step Four

Begin with 32 strands and lay one on either side of the dot. Pull the threads gently into the slits.

Step Five

Cross the disk straight across and insert one thread into each slit on each side of the black dot on the number 16. Maintain sufficient strain on the strands to keep the knot in the middle of the disk's hole.

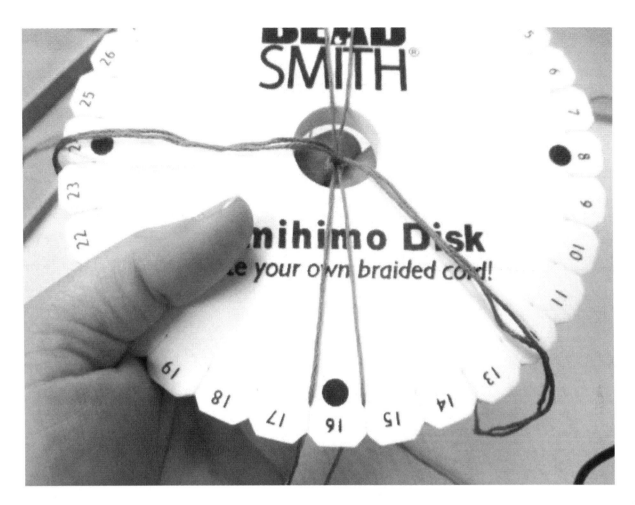

Step Six

At the right of the disk, insert one strand into each of the openings on each side of the black dot on the number 8.

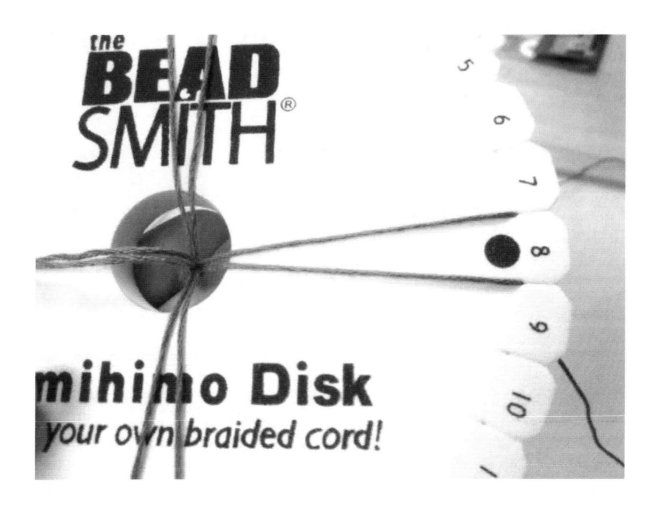

Step Seven

Proceed to the disk's left side and insert one strand into each of the slits on each side of this black dot on number 24. After you've secured all of the cables, your disk should look like this. Keep in mind that the knot remains centered.

Beginning The Braid

Please keep in mind that when we refer to a numbered slit, we are referring to the slit immediately to the left of that number.

You may want to retain some weight behind the knot at the disk's center, particularly at the beginning of the braid, to maintain a tight, consistent appearance as you go. You may accomplish this by hand, holding the knot end and gradually pushing down as you go, but it may be quicker to secure the knot using a tiny bag containing twenty-five cents. This allows both hands to be used for braiding.

Step Eight

Begin by extending the rope in split 17 straight up and over the disk

to slit 31.

Step Nine: Continue over the disk with cable 1 until you reach slit 15. Bear in mind to maintain the same amount of tension throughout the braid to ensure an even braid free of bumps.

Step Ten: Take a 1/4 turn clockwise on the Kumihimo disk. At this point, the black positioning dot at number 24 should be at the top.

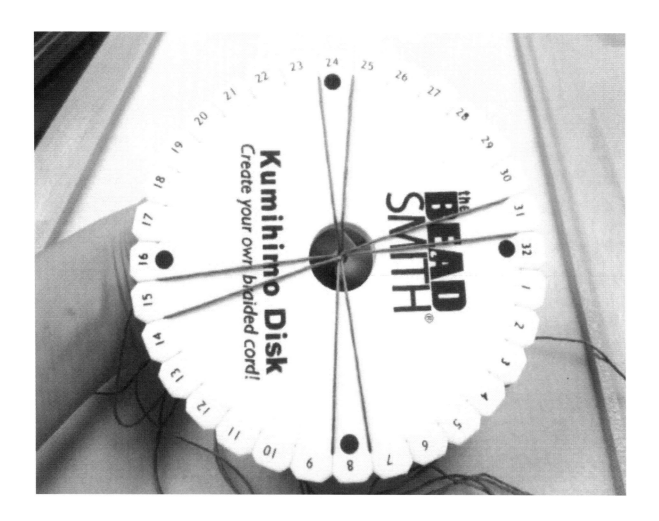

Step Eleven: Move cord 9 to slit 23 and bear in mind to maintain tension on the threads.

Step Twelve: Continue across chord 25 to slit 7.

Step Thirteen: Turn the disc one quarter clockwise to reach the next set of cables. As you can see, you are essentially repeating steps two through four for each chord combination (up and left, down and right). After a few laps around the disk, the numbers become irrelevant.

Step Fourteen: Repeat steps two through four until the desired length is obtained. The length depends depend on the design and the procedure used to finish the ends.

Step Fifteen: Remove the braid from the disk and secure the unfinished end with a knot.

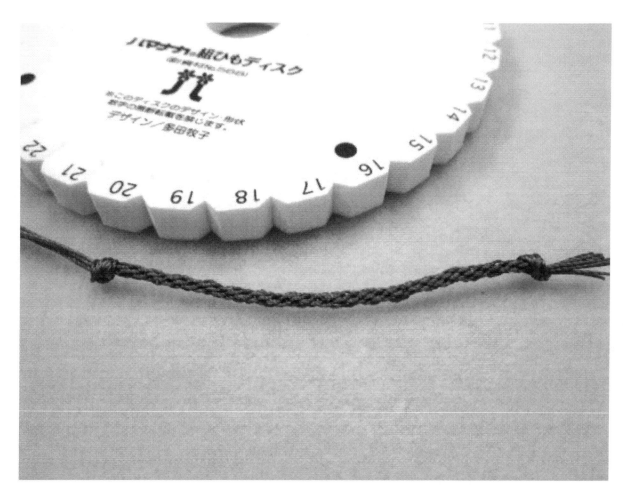

Step Sixteen: Tie a knot towards the end of the Kumihimo braid using Nymo D string.

Step Seventeen: Wrap one end of the Nymo as tightly as possible around the braid. Wrap the Nymo in the opposite direction as the initial wrap.

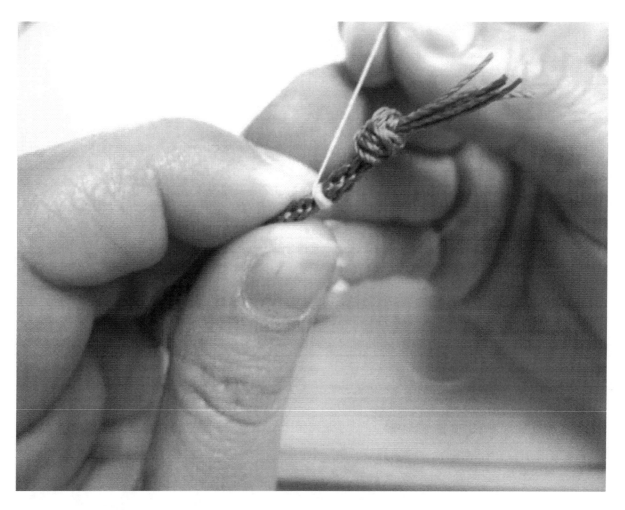

Step Eighteen: Tie another knot in the Nymo and burn the surplus thread using a thread burner.

Step Nineteen: Cut the braid's knot.

Step Twenty: Cut the end of the braid to a length that will contain your end clap. In the picture below, a crimp end with a loop is used.

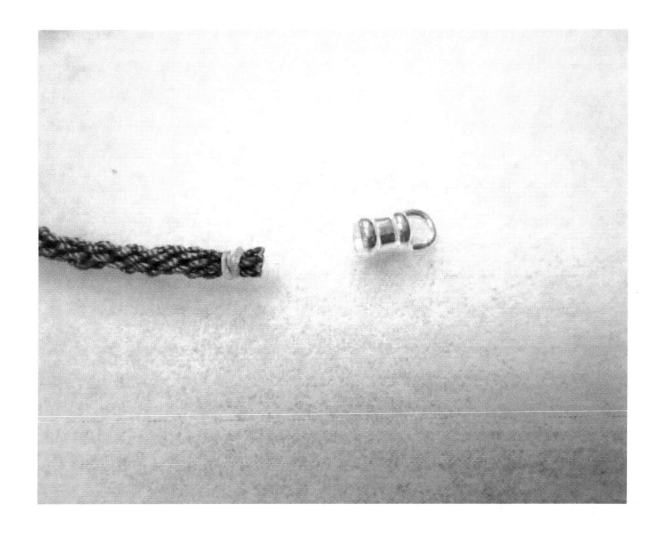

Step Twenty Three: To cover the Nymo thread, slide the crimp end over the end of the braid and crimp with a set of chain nose pliers.

Wow! Your 8 strand kumihibo spiral braid is ready. This can be use to make a beaded necklace or bracelets which will be demontrated in the next chapter.

Having known how to go about the 8 strands, lets proceed to making a 12 strand spiral kumihimo braid. Ready?

CHAPTER FOUR

Making a 12 Strand Spiral Kumihimo Braid

And, as it turns out, the spiral with 12 strands is just as simple as the 8 strands and you can make as much as four of it in a night cos it's so so simple.

Now Let's get started!

Materials and Tools You Need

- A round kumihimo disk
- 2mm Cords of different colours of your choice. The colours used in this tutorial are yellow and pink(.Yellow as the outer colour and pink as the inner colour).
- A pair of scissors

Procedures

- Make four cuttings of your inner color of about 39 inches long and two cuttings of your outer color of about 45 inches long.

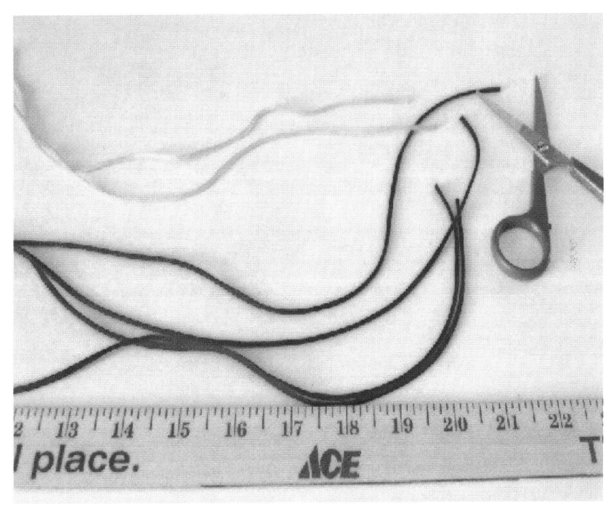

- Put the ends of the cords together and locate the center. Then and secure with a strong knot.

- Pass the knot through the front of the disk.

- Lace the disk as shown below

Let the inner colour go on each side of the disk marked 2, 14, 18, and 30.

While the outer colour will go on each side of disk marked 8 and 24.

We're going to split the disk in half horizontally, left and right.

- Take the bottom left chord and put it to the left of the top left cord on the left side.
- Place the top right cable to the right of the bottom left cord.
- Take the cable on the bottom left and put it to the left of the top left chord on the right side.

- Place the top right chord to the right of the bottom right cable left.
- Rotate the disk and reposition the bottom left cable to the left of the top left chord.
- Place the top right cable to the right of the sole cord remaining on the bottom.
- Turn the disk and repeat the pattern.

Your cable will begin to emerge from the rear as you work the disk.

When you've reached the desired length, grasp all of the cords and squeeze them together to prevent them from unraveling on you and remove it carefully from the disk.

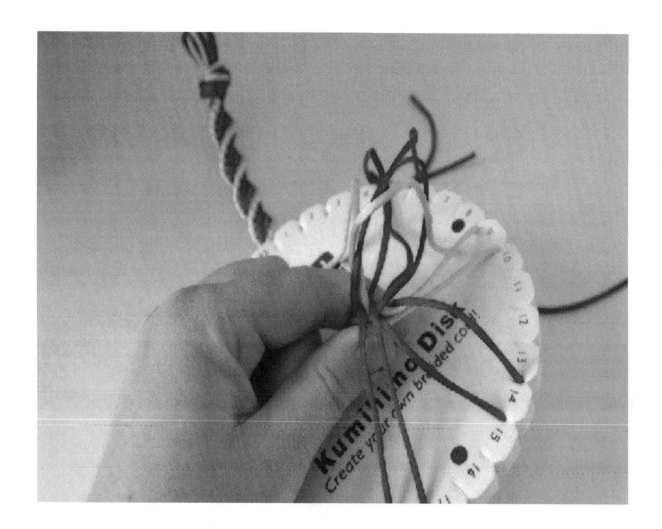

• Secure the end with a knot.

- Tie the ends through the knot, similar to how you would with a standard friendship bracelet.
- Bonded the knot in place ensuring that glue is placed both within and around the knot and make sure that the glue dries clearly.

Take the raw ends and ignite them with a lighter. It just takes a split second, but this will secure the ends and prevent them from unraveling.Make sure that the cord is not flammable.

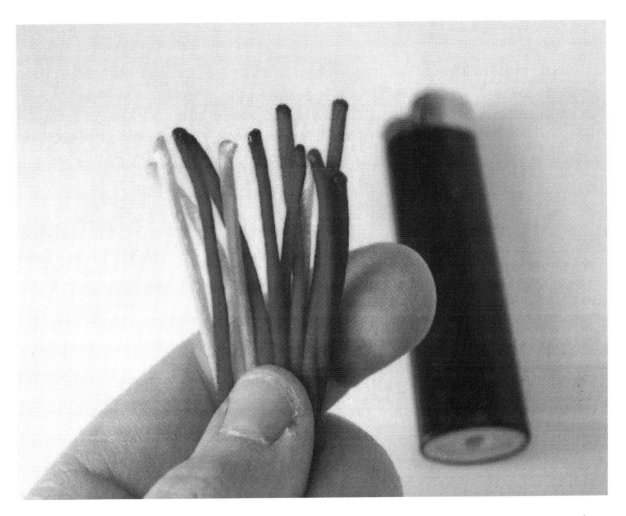

Due to the fact that the knots are bounded in place, you can wear it as a bangle and just put it on your wrist.

I hope you had fun going through this tutorial.

Do well to experiment it with different colours and see the beauty of it.

Up next is the making of flat braid Kumihimo.

CHAPTER FIVE

HOW TO MAKE FLAT BRAID KUMIHIMO

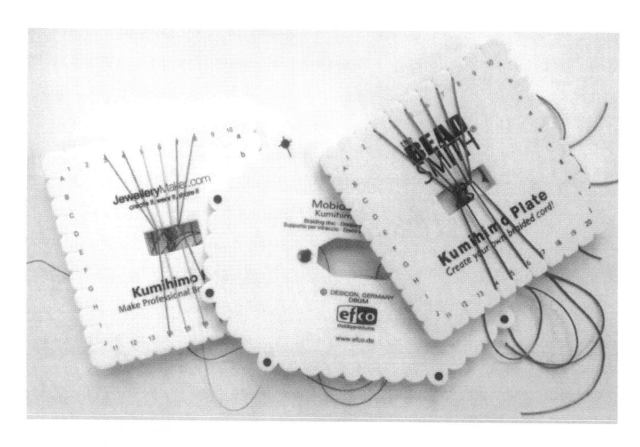

10 Cord Flat Braid with a Chevron Design

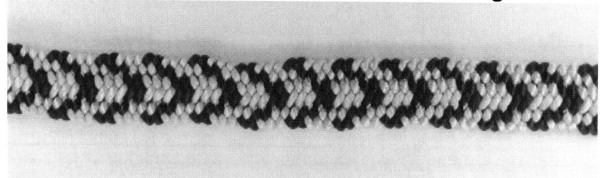

This is the most often used flat braid design since it is simple to learn and results in a functional flat braid. By alternating colors, you may make V and X-shaped shapes in the braid. This may also be created with 14 or 18 cords, however maintaining a uniform tension would be more challenging with that many cords.

Getting Started

- Insert six cords into slots 3,4,5,6,7, and 8 on the top of the disk; and then four cords in slots 14,15,16, and 17 on the bottom of the disk.

- Remove the cord in slot 5 and place it in slot e and the also the cord in slot 6 to slot E.

- Begin with the wires on the left side of the plate. Carry out the following movements of cords:15 to 5, 4 to15, 14 to 4, and 3 to 14

- Then on the right side of the plate, carry out the following movements of cords: 16 to 6, 7 to16, 17 to 7,

and 8 to 17

- Transfer the cord from slot E to slot 3 then from slot e to slot 8.

This will bring the cords back to their initial position. Then continue with the steps shown above until the braid reaches the length you desire.

It is advisable to practice this braid numerous times before commencing on a specific piece of jewelry, since equal tension is necessary for the braid to have straight edges. The transitions from 5 to e and 6 to E are critical because they determine the breadth of the braid. The more they are drawn up, the finer the braid becomes. Consistency in these movements results in an equal breadth and straight sides.

It's enjoyable to play with various color placements to produce different results.

CHAPTER SIX

MAKING KUMIHIMO WITH BEADS

Once you've mastered the fundamentals of creating a Kumihimo braid, you'll almost certainly want to experiment with adding beads to the braid. This requires a bit more preparation time before you begin, but the results are well worth the effort. When developing your design, take in mind that the ultimate product will vary according to the color scheme, the size of the beads, and the number of beaded strands used. Additionally, keep in mind that the stringing material size will be decided by the hole size of the beads you want to use.

Instructions to Making a beaded 8 Strand circular kumihimo

- Determine the desired length of braid first. As a general guideline, cut the stringing material three times the required length. This should suit the majority of designs, even those including beads.
- Following that, you'll need to establish the quantity of beads required. On all eight strands, we're using TOHO beads in size 8/0.

Then, proceed with the following steps:

#1: String one bead and then work your way back up through it to make a stopper bead. Do this procedure for all eight strands.

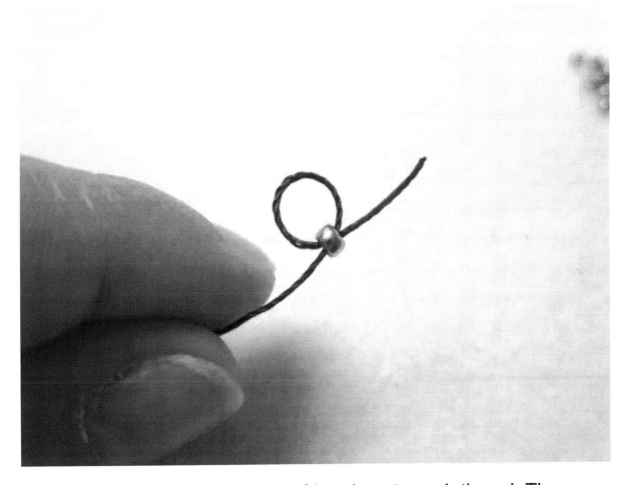

#2: String the required number of beads onto each thread. Then wind each strand of beads onto its own bobbin, leaving the open stringing end exposed.

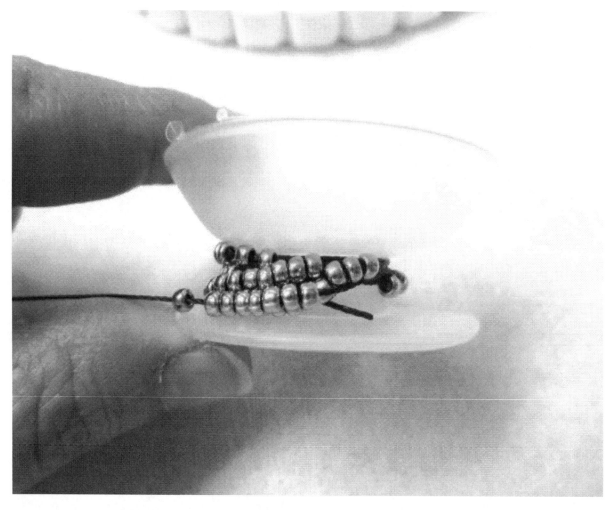

#3: Tie all the eight strands open stringing ends together in a knot.

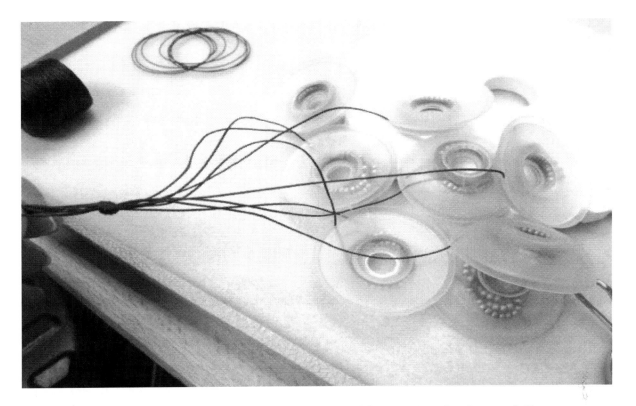

 # 4: Place the knot in the Kumihimo disk's center hole and the strings in the slots on each side of the placement dots.

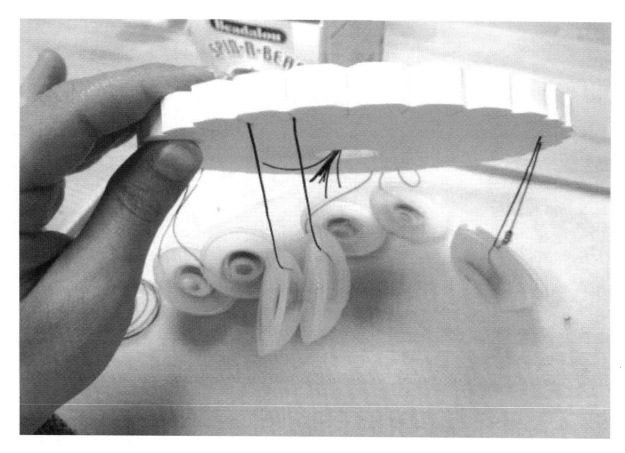

This is how your Kumihimo disk should appear.

 # 5: Braid about half inch of braid without adding beads. Without beads in this portion, it will be simpler to tie the end when it comes time to complete the braid.

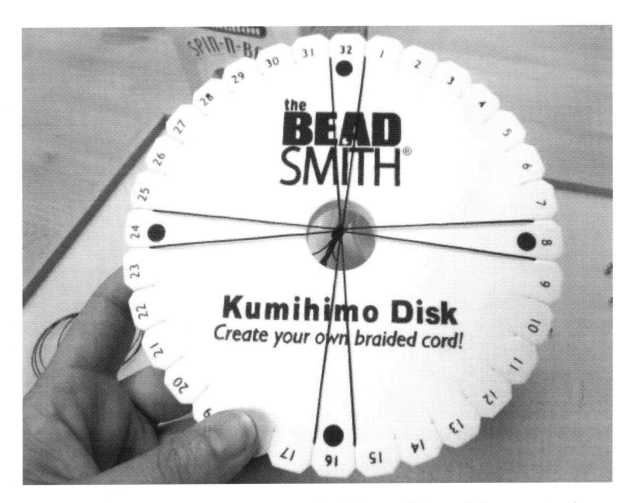

 # 6: Take a few beads from each bobbin and thread them onto the strands, then shut the bobbins.

Braiding instructions are same whether beads are used or not. The only difference is that if you're using beads, you'll need to insert one bead into the braid for each strand as you go. Take note that the first few beads may seem jumbled. They should balance out as you advance as long as you remember to maintain proper string tension while working.

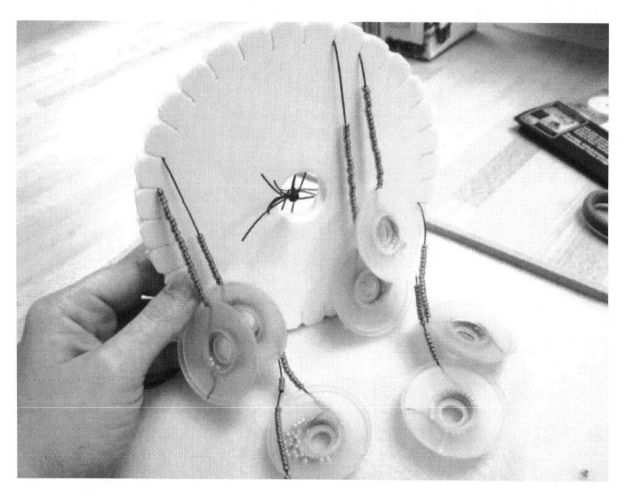

 # 8: Extricate warp 17 from the slit and thread one bead onto the string. Slide the bead as far as possible.Make sure it rests under warp 24.

 # 9: Raise warp 17 and insert it into slit 31.

 # 10: slid up one bead onto warp 1 and let it rest under wrap 8.

 # 11: Reduce warp 1 to slit 15.

#12: Turn the Kumihimo disk one quater turn clockwise, or 90 degrees, until the dot between slots 8 and 9 is on the bottom. Then bring one bead onto warp 9 until it is positioned under warp 15.

#13:Remove warp 9 and place it in slit 23.

#14: Bring 1 bead up onto warp 25 to continue this design. Drop warp 25 into slit 7 such that the bead rests just below warp 31.

#15: Make a one-quarter turn clockwise on the disk and slide 1 bead onto warp 32. Then, move warp 32 over to slit 14.

#16 :Fix 1 bead to warp 16 and move it to slit 30. Then make a clockwise one-quarter turn on the disk.

#17: Continue in this manner until the required length is obtained. Do not include the half inch of unbeaded braid in your total length, since it will be cut off.

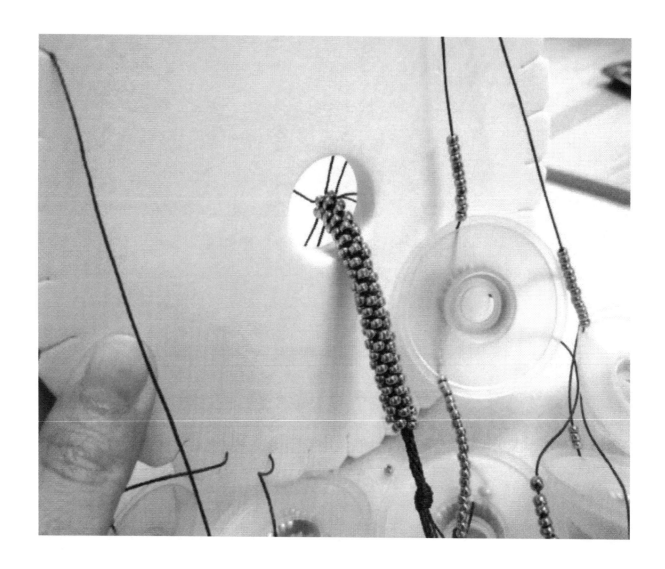

#18: Make an additional half inch of plain braid.

#19: Remove the braid from the disk and make a knot in the ends of all eight strands.

#20: To Fix a crimp at the end, cut a length of Nymo D thread and secure one end of the braid with a knot.

Wrap one end of the Nymo tightly around the braid several times and then repeat with the other end moving in the opposite direction.

Secure with another knot and then trim the extra thread with a thread

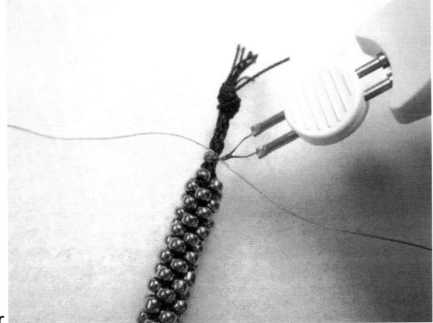

burner.

#21: Trim off the end of the braid

#22: Cover the end with a crimp end to conceal the Nymo and then crimp with a pair of chain nose pliers.

#23: To Add End Caps to a kumihimo braid, continue wrapping the braid with Nymo as instructed before. This is an excellent moment to measure the end and determine the appropriate size end cap. Bear in mind the length of the braid's end, as you want it to stretch all the way to the very tip of the endcap for a tight grasp. It is better to leave the end long and then test your end cap to ensure it fits properly. Reduce the length more if necessary until the fit is right.

#24: Apply a little amount of glue to the interior of the endcap and the braid's end and fix the endcaps on the braid ends as far as possible and then allow it to dry.

.

Here you have your beaded kumihimo which can be worn as a bracelet or a necklace depending on the length.

Conclusion

I am super sure that you find this book educating and interesting as you have learnt the basis of kumihimo. I encourage you to keep repeating the guidlines contained in this book and in no time you will be a professional in KUMIHIMO.

Cheers!